WHAT'S
GOING ON?

JANET BROWN

authorHOUSE®

AuthorHouse™ LLC
1663 Liberty Drive
Bloomington, IN 47403
www.authorhouse.com
Phone: 1-800-839-8640

Published by AuthorHouse   07/10/2014

ISBN: 978-1-4969-2429-2 (sc)
ISBN: 978-1-4969-2428-5(e)

Library of Congress Control Number: 2014911943

This book is a continuation to my previous one entitled "Young But Old" sequel. It entails the next stages in life that encompass the latter years of a teenager through to becoming an almost seasoned woman. The times in life that are so colorful and unexplainable and we think we know everything but don't have a clue! The times in life when we have all the answers "so we think"! Trying to establish ourselves on our way to becoming an adult within our own identities, questionable friendships, dating and where we plan on going in life. This is a walk through my eyes as a teen and pre—adult but applies to everyone in general. Also, dedicated to my two daughters Laqualla Dunn and Chitaria Dunn in hopes that this will further answer your teen questions on where you are currently in life and what's to come. I'm hoping that you grasp most of what I'm trying to teach you through my mistakes and informational journey.

Contents

Look Ahead

To all who read this, I want you
to observe and also know,
Things happen accordingly to
how you let them go,
Don't get it mixed up and
don't take me wrong,
We've all at one point or another
sang that sad sad song,
But as you get older and more
mature in the mind,
You start to put the minor
life problems behind,
You look at life in a broad
and spacious sight,
Looking toward the future and
you now see the light,
No matter what people say
or even do to you,

Only you can determine
your future; only you,
So those that have heard, I'm going
to say this and just be done,
Do what you need to in life but
don't forget to have fun,
I am done for now and have
said what must be said,
Stop looking behind you and
start looking ahead!

Problems

Do you sometimes feel that
things aren't right?
Every day you wake up, you have to fight?
Fight for things that you thought
were already yours,
But someone else is always
trying to make them theirs,
So many things will happen in life,
Sometimes but not all they turn out all right,
If there are things that you
feel you can't handle,
Move around and just change that channel,
It seems bad things only
happen if you do wrong,
So always keep things in
order where they belong,
Problems can occur because of
the path that you chose,

So try to do the best in whatever
it is that you do,
When things are wrong just
try to stop and solve em,
You can't ever live without
enduring some problems!

What is Love?

The question is; what is love?
Is it something that's sent from above?
Sometimes love can be all so good,
If everyone shared love alike it would,
If you ask me this; what do I mean?
Love controls life and everything in between,
Love is for you and also me,
It's only to be shared exclusively,
Dealing with love you have to just be kind,
Don't put hateful things on your mind,
I guess love appears to be alright for now,
Until everyone gets the
concept and learns how,
Just remove the pain of the
hurt and that grudge,
And tell everyone the answer to what is love?

Caught Up

There is this guy that I really really like,
But he only come comes
around very late at night,
I gave myself to him for a hot lil minute,
But he belonged to her from
the very beginning,
He erased the pain that I had once felt,
But the pain that he left didn't quite help,
I just wanted him to be my ole man,
But all he wanted was a cutter friend,
When I was younger I didn't
really understand this,
How all this got started from
a single little kiss,
How boys mislead girls and lead us on,
When it all boils down they end up gone,
They leave you stuck to feel
that stinging burn,

You're left there alone with
just a lesson to learn,
Everyone goes through problems
but in a different way,
But hold your head up dear because
there's still the next day,
Men will put you through things
and you might as well know,
If you can't take the mess
its best you let him go,
Take it from me I've been
dealt with such luck,
Stop while you can before
you get caught up!!

How could you let go so easily?

We started out being the perfect
couple for a while,
Everyone was hating and
jocking our love style,
We were doing very well and
a stone got in the way,
Then something else happened
and we began to go astray,
We began to lose love and drift
away one from the other,
But the feelings we had we
could never seem to cover,
Relationships will have problems
I know this for a fact,
But is seems no matter what
you always came back,
We had a few fights and
also some arguments,

So we lost the love that we
thought God had sent,
I lost a love that I once had in my life,
Cause it seems that men leave
without even thinking twice,
I'd think with a special one
you'd never be torn apart,
Because true love comes from
deep within the heart,
I have yet to figure out a man
and for now it beats me,
How could they just let go of love so easily?

Why End it like this?

We began a relationship but
jumped into it kind of fast,
All could've figured out that
this thing wouldn't last,
I at the time was married and
you also had a girl,
It just so happened we were a
part of the same world,
I wanted to be with you and
you also with me,
So we made a few changes
and together were we,
We shouldn't have rushed into
it but took a lil more slow,
So the inner part of each other
we could learn to show,
I believed you were different and
I swore you were the one,

But you proved to me that you
are just another son of a gun,
We left it alone without one
last hug or a kiss,
To say we were in love why
would you end it like this?

?

I know I'm not alone because
none of us understand,
Why we endure so much when
we choose to love a man,
All we want to do is give
them the very best of us,
But they do us so wrong and
begin to lose your trust,
But we try to maintain in hopes
that the love is strong,
There is no excuse when they
choose to do us wrong,
People try to warn us and
try to lead us right,
So why don't we ever heed any of this advice?

Though we are suffering and
wanting to move on,
We remain still right behind
them tagging along,
But who's to say anything

?

Uncontent

Sometimes I just lay around
all by myself alone,
Justifying and knowing that my
life won't last very long,
And I feel my life is very
twisted, tied and bent,
But yet and still I remain uncontent,
Blaming myself and others for
the things that I let go on,
My emotions of rage and bad
luck have became full blown,
For all those wrong things in my
life that have caused a dent,
But yet and still I remain uncontent,
The pain and heartache inside
me will forever linger,

After all the events that have
come I still point a finger,
I feel as an orphan child, who
has been shipped and sent,
But yet and still I remain uncontent!

Agony

Why do we live in such misery?
Why do people always
wanna screw over me?
Why is everything so jacked up?
Every filthy man just wants a touch,
Young girls running around coochy poppin,
With all this drama why not try stoppin,
Nobody anywhere ever gives a shit,
Long as they can get them a lil bit,
All these people that live in this hood,
Nobody here seems to be any good,
Nobody here wants anything out of life,
All they care about is the
streets and getting high,
Everybody wants to see you stay down,
When you begin to make it
they wanna clown,

People are scared of what you might do,
I should know because I've been there too,
But I'm ready to end this useless debris,
And put an end to my hood agony!

Strange and Unknown

One day I sat and just
glared up into the sky,
Wondering what's going on here and why,
Every day I want to leave this
selfish, chaotic world,
Because I feel so useless
and fragile as a girl,
When I ask our Father
what it is that he does,
He says he's changing it, that's how it was,
I pray to the Lord our Father every day,
That he'll change this place and our evil way,
After all I've been through
I'm just hovering along,
My mind holds on to things that
are still strange and unknown!

So Many Things

There are so many things that I
didn't want to go through,
But it went on anyway there's
nothing that I could do,
There are also many things
that I live now to regret,
Like some of those fools in life that I met,
I wish I could start over and
correct all of my mistakes,
But if life were that easy we'd
all take that piece of cake,
I wish I could go somewhere
and be away from humanity,
So I could just be Janet and
it won't be embarrassing,
Every day I wonder what
the next day will bring,
And why do I have to put
up with so many things!

Lost Hopes

God I'm asking that you please
reach out your hand,
I really need to know in life where I stand,
I need your support to improve
what is to come in my destiny,
Tell me, is everything going
on just a test for me?
I'm having hopes of going
just a little bit higher,
But it's not what I want but
what is of your desire,
I live everyday as if it's a surprise,
But I ask in turn to wake up
daily just a little more wise,
I wish for once that something
falls in perspective,
I need to search deeper inside
as so does a detective,

To stop things from always going downhill,
To find what it is that I long
for; one day I hope I will,
My life goes like no ordinary soaps,
But is only full of a bunch of lost hopes!

When I sit Here Alone

When I sit here alone all by myself,
I try to escape the stress of everyone else,
I think of all the things that
I did to others so wrong,
And all the chaos of this
planet that does go on,
I look to the future but look
to the past again,
Hoping time will bring all
of my pain to an end,
I wonder why people can't
ever just get along,
And my life is hell why have
I been here so long?
When I sit here I look up
and stare into the sky,
Not asking the Lord but
asking myself why?

I try to live everyday and pay it no attention,
But you can't live here on this earth
without another's bad intentions,
I wonder if this is the place
where I really belong,
These are some of the things I
think of when I sit here alone!

God's Great Gift

Everyone should fall down on their knee,
And say out loudly Lord
I'm ready to receive,
Tell the Lord you're ready
to accept and endure,
The things that he has to offer for evermore,
You'll learn how to overcome temptation,
And all other things of that relation,
Ask the lord to send you a vision,
Now's the time to make that decision,
Do you want everlasting life and love?
And the things that are
offered only from above,
Or do you want to burn way
below the ground?
With the demons and hellfire all around,
God gave us our arms to give away a hug,
And some people don't even have that much,

Down here on earth we have it rough,
But God will send for us
when he feels it's enough,
Call on God when you need that lift,
To receive the love in God's Great Gift!

The First Time

I used to love this man, but he
wouldn't love me back,
He wanted one thing from
me and that was that,
I wanted him to understand me
and what I wanted from him,
But he would never listen to me
or leave alone the rest of them,
I tried to teach this man that one
good woman is all you need,
But as time went on I felt like
I wasn't his woman indeed,
He used to say he loved me
and no one else but me,
While there was always someone
else in the shadows still lurking,
Men are just so greedy and
want to have us all,

Until that one day when they'll
have their own downfall,
One woman that breaks them from
the game that all love to play,
It is then that they change their
minds only then on that day,
And then they want to understand the
woman that has left them behind,
When all they ever had to do is
get it right the first time!

Emotions

What are emotions and are they for real?
Is it a mental thing or is it
something that you can feel?
When someone says they love you,
can you believe what they say?
Should you have a cold heart and not
let your feelings get in the way?
Once you've been hurt is that a
bitter feeling or is it an emotion?
Does it take a while for you to put
your heart back into motion?
Should you always protect yourself
and build a cage around your heart?
Where do all of your feelings or
emotions fall on this chart?
Are you happy when you get that
special warm feeling inside?

Are you sad when you're hurt
and it shows on the outside?
Do you panic when you're lost
and don't know what to do?
Are you in fear when
something frightens you?
Do you feel grief when you
lose someone dear?
Are you in shame when there's
something about you that you hear?
Have you been surprised when
something unexpected happens?
Do you feel wonder when
things start snappin?
Do you anticipate when something
is going to be real big?
Are you in shock when that
ship actually comes in?
Do you feel in distress when you
can't control the situation?

When do you get the courage
to keep on pacin?
Do you feel disgust when
you're let down again?
Have you ever felt the love of
God, Savior and Friend?

It Keeps Happening to Me

Why is it that every time I find
someone that I would like to keep?
He's always the wrong one and
it takes me so long to see?
I waste the years trying to make a
relationship that can never be,
Because I want to be with one man
but they want me plus 2 and 3,
At the end of the road when I find
that it's time for me to now go on,
I end up singing that "another
one bites the dust" song,
For once in my life I hope to find
a one that is meant for Janet,
But more and more I begin to realize
there is no one that exists on this planet,

And for such a long time have those
apples have fallen so far from my tree,
And when I think I've caught one, there
it goes again; it keeps happening to me!

Confused

Have you ever felt like you don't
really know how to feel?
Like everything always has
to be a big ordeal?
At times do you feel kind of out of place?
Like you're still at the beginning,
not the end of the race?
Does everyone always neglect and doubt you?
Like they know exactly what
you're going to do?
Do you ever have these unlikely feelings?
Like you're the one who's always illing?
Do you ever feel like you're
constantly being used?
Is it all in my mind? Am I just confused?

Unstable love Affair

Once someone special said that he loved me,
The way he showed it tho goes accordingly,
He was always withal of his other girls,
Sometimes it made me so
sick I wanted to hurl,
But over and over he says he wants only me,
And I believed him so foolishly,
He always put his other
girls and friends first,
While I'm left here alone
to feel at my worst,
He lives as if he has not one real care,
I hate this damn stupid unstable love affair.

He's not Mine

There's someone that I want
to be with very bad,
In fact he's one that I've already had,
I wanted to go a little bit further,
I want him only and shall
settle for no other,
Not to my surprise he's already taken,
From the start I must've been mistaken,
A man like him doesn't ever settle down,
The list begins at one and runs all around,
I tried to explain to him my deepest feelings,
And he just stared and me
and started giggling,
He took it as if it was some sort of joke,
That very minute I felt like
my heart got broke,
I knew right then I was just being played,

So I had to let my feelings
just sort of sway,
I can't blame him because
there's a many of his kind,
But I can't deal with it if He's not Mine.

At Times

At times I sit here all by myself,
And I don't know what to do,
My heart is like an empty shelf,
And it's all because of a dude,
He left me here with a broken heart,
And it should've been a sin,
He's hurt me since the very start,
And I still went back again,
I'm shook up so bad inside,
And I feel so left alone,
I'm here to sigh and lose my pride,
For the days that he was gone,
But I tell you this to let you know,
That one day he'll want to be mine,
But I'll go on to find a new soul,
And then he'll be left behind,

I try to speak on this, so that it may happen,
Because he committed so many a crime,
Stop the drooling here's a napkin,
This is how I feel at times.

Men

Ladies, why is it that some of our men,
Say they love us but continue to
mistreat us again and again,
And all they do is lie,
And couldn't love even if
they actually did try,
They put us through lots of stuff,
Until they believe that we've had enough,
But when you two are alone,
When everyone else is already gone,
They'll tell you lots of things,
Some of it we even think that they mean,
But when other people seem to come along,
They act like the feelings
were not that strong,

Because they never really
meant what they said,
They were only trying to buck up our head,
They'll try to use you again and again,
Don't you love those stupid men?

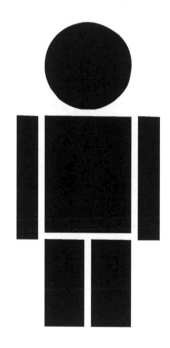

Only when you're Horny

Only when you're horny, you
want to call on me,
When you do call me you
ask for that one thing,
You have so many girls that
are flipped out over you,
You try to lie to me but it
shows in all that you do,
It's happened so much and
I'm crushed because of,
I don't care anymore cause you're
beginning to lose my love,
You've pushed me away again and again,
All the time I'm thinking
I'm your lady friend,

I thought you were mine and
I was your one and only,
But now it's clear to me that you
only call when you're horny.

Love is Born

When things in life get really rough,
When laughter sometimes just isn't enough,
There's something that can lift up that spirit,
Just holding to you close
the one that's dearest,
Some things in life may bring you down,
But you'll be alright if loves around,
Love your someone and make it clear,
And hold them to your heart very near,
Give you love to them every day,
So from their mouth you'll hear them say,
Honey I love you and tell
them you love them back,
You're a lover now not a mack,
Open your heart and give love a chance,
Love will help your relationship enhance,
When that organ inside gets
bright red and warm,
Be prepared because love is born.

When no one's Around

When no one's around he's all just for me,
When people come around he
says I'm mistaken see,
When no one's around it's only the two of us,
When people come around all we do is fuss,
When we are alone we're all lovey–dovey,
But when people come around he
says that I'm stupid and ugly,
When no one's around he's
smiling all in my grill,
When people come around he says
that the feelings weren't real,
When no one's around he treats
me like his treasure,
When people come around he asks
what I can do to give him pleasure,
When no one's around he's
stuck to me like glue,

When people come around he
says I can't help you boo,
When no one's around that's
when our relationship begins,
But when people come around
we are just friends,
When no one's around we
can always get down,
Oh how things change when
no one's around!

Come With Me

I'm asking please want you take my hand,
I want to take you to my home land,
To me, I think you're one of the best,
In my heart, you rise above all the rest,
The friendship we have can
become a lil more realer,
If you place me as the higher superior,
I want to be listed above them all,
The love I have for you remains uncalled,
Needing you to be one with me,
I'll show you what real love should be,
Many people don't realize until it's too late,
Decreasing the active love rate,
You try to stunt and just make green,
Knowing that you still need
a true thug queen,
I'll be that and for you whatever I shall be,
But first you must take my
hand and come with me.

Feelings I can't Explain

There are some feelings all
bunched up in my head,
Although sometimes I wish I were dead,
Feelings boggled inside my
pinched down soul,
I try to let them out to keep myself whole,
My feelings sometimes
bombard me all at once,
Then more and more just adds to the punch,
I'm going crazy and this I know,
Believe you, me I'm right at the dow,
When I was younger I
should have learned then,
That falling in traps of evil
that love may never win,
I guess I am the only one to blame,
For these impeccable feelings I can't explain.

Who does he Love?

Listen girls there's something
I want you to know,
So check this script out down below,
There are male out there just to confuse,
If you have one let him go or you'll lose,
All they'll do is just hurt your feelings,
So with their dumb ass don't keep on dealing,
He uses you for nothing
but whenever he can,
But you still hold on thinking
he's the right man,
He tells you this but everyone else that,
All the time he's just stabbing
you in your back,
It's happening to you now but
you don't know what to do,
He says he loves you but
tells who else that too,

Today's changing as with every other day,
And he'll leave you if you don't
play the game his way,
When you're alone he says what
he thinks you want to know,
But he only tells you these
things so that you won't go,
And also when you're alone
he's all in your face,
You not knowing that you and
her are running a race,
A race to see who can lock him down first,
And the other women are left
there also being hurt,
So you try to move on cause
you know you can't win,
Finding another man and
then it happens again,

You're looking for someone who
can fit you like a glove,
Asking yourself the whole
time who does he love?

Why

Someone tell this answer please,
Why do I get forsaken when I'm offering?
I give my love to be taken seriously,
But they only want to test me you see,
I keep him special to me no
matter what he may do,
I'll always be there with the
feelings still so true,
I'm saying I'll stay around
do I make myself clear,
Because the love we shared I
hold to my heart so near,
But men take love as a weakness
and treat us so cruel,
But continually stating that
they're so real and true,
They only lie, never stating
how they really feel,

Knowing that with love they can never deal,
So the true feelings they will continue to hide,
Until they truly let go of their selfish pride,
They will always state what
they will and can do,
But their promise they never hold on to,
So until that day you consistently sigh,
Still asking yourself the question of why?

Someone let me Know

There's this question that I
can't seem to understand,
As you know by reading some of my
other poems this is about a man,
Why is it when in love, one
always seem to be misused?
We offer our love but they
always seem to refuse,
This question remains boggling
deep in my mind,
In me why can't a man confine all his time?
Is it that love is something
that's hard to figure?
Is it like a gun to their head
with the hand on the trigger?
Men trip on love and are amazed at the thing,
Because they are only looking
for that nightly fling,

Laughing at the others that play their part,
Cracking jokes about someone
giving away their heart,
Love is something that men
can't seem to comprehend,
That there can be a special bond
between men and women,
Tell them its okay just open
up and let it flow,
What's wrong with love
someone let me know!

Won't Leave but Can't Stay

Boy I really don't understand you,
I try to be a good woman for you,
I want to please you in every way I can,
Sometimes you treat me less than a woman,
I love you and state it very clear,
But how can it show, if you're never here,
I'm never asking you for nothing,
Cause all I really need is your loving,
I'm there for you whenever you need me,
I'm more woman than any man can need,
I do my best to keep my man happy,
I try not to argue or even get sassy,
I'm here for you as a soul mate,
I'm here for you to love and
no thoughts of hate,
I try to explain and help you understand,

And there you go again acting
like a stubborn man,
We go through the same type
of shit each and every day,
I won't leave but can't stay!

A Heart that can't be Healed

I know many of you out there can relate,
Being in a relationship with
no love but so much hate,
I tried to do my part and also make it work,
While the whole time he's
chasing behind another skirt,
I fell in love at a very young age;
at least I thought I did,
When I really knew nothing,
cause I was just a kid,
People tried to warn me and
let me know up front,
That's not the type of love
that you should want,
I was being hard-headed
and tried to be grown,
When I really didn't know
what was going on,

They told me I wasn't ready and
didn't know what I was doing,
Me not understanding that this was
a beginning of a great ruin,
Momma tried to be straight with
me and tried to keep it real,
Now, I'm stuck with a heart
that can't be healed.

Sometime

Many things men do I have
yet to understand,
Sometimes you'll admit that you're my man,
But I don't want to seem insecure,
But at times I feel you're not so sure,
Instead of you loving me
and making me happy,
You can never be there for me,
Like those times I've been there for you,
You've left me here feeling through,
I sit here alone awaiting your arrival,
I'm keeping myself in a total denial,
As you're out there running the street,
As I play along and let you cheat,
Now I believe it's time for me to wake-up,
I'm praying I can get out
and not remain stuck,
Before I lose my own time in life,

When I can become another man's wife,
As I'm to say that my own
love had me blind,
Sometime we just have to let go
and wake up sometime!

Hi my name is Janet Brown; I am a 32 year old mother of two beautiful and wonderful daughters LaQualla and Chitaria Dunn. I was born in a small town of Hammond, Louisiana about 45 minutes from the live city of New Orleans, La and 35 minutes from Baton Rouge where I lived out most of my life. I inspired to be a model at age 11 and began that long journey. I began to write poetry at age 14 and continuing.

I was raised with my mother along with two other sisters (me being the eldest had most of the responsibilities); being very grateful for that because it taught me and helped mold me to be the woman that I am today. I was brought up in church with my dad and try to keep GOD center in my life. All who know me know that my children are my life!

At age 17 I entered into a competition i.e. International swimsuit competition with Venus Swimsuit Model Competition, Unique International where I won 2nd place out of 1500 women in the state. My mom told me that I had to stay in school so I postponed my dreams. Throughout my adolescent years I loved to laugh, act, sing and tell jokes but I was shy. As I got older I going through school I participated in things such as choir, arts and anything creative. I soon learned that I had an artistic, creative niche for my life. I love to entertain and be a part of the entertainment. I am very proactive in the community and my church life. I have been in the world of modeling/acting since 1997. In 2011, I was an extra in many films i.e. Ray with Jamie Foxx, GCB with Christen Chenoweth. I've also been a part of several stage plays i.e. 2 Men and & 7 Women, Jesus is Love Stage Play, Shreveport Santa Stage Play.

I have been working in healthcare areas ranging from emergency room to quality assurance now for about 15 years. I am an IBO self employed Entrepreneur, an employee of Methodist Systems, notary, aspiring poet, model, actress, and transcriptionist just to name a few things. I enjoy working with and entertaining people and I love to laugh and have fun.

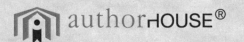

ISBN 978-1-4969-2429-2

51295

9 781496 924292